IKIGAI
& The 53ʳᵈ CARD

It Ain't Over Till the Last Card is Played

IKIGAI
& The 53rd CARD

Dr. REET

It Ain't Over Till the Last Card is Played

Worldwide Published by
Pendown Press

PENDOWN PRESS

An ISO 9001 & ISO 14001 Certified Co.,

Regd. Office: 2525/193, 1st Floor, Onkar Nagar-A,
Tri Nagar, Delhi-110035
Ph.: 09350849407, 09312235086
E-mail: info@pendownpress.com
Branch Office: 1A/2A, 20, Hari Sadan, Ansari Road,
Daryaganj, New Delhi-110002
Ph.: 011-45794768
Website: PendownPress.com

First Edition: 2020

ISBN: 978-93-90479-46-7

Layout and Cover Designed by Pendown Graphics Team

Printed and Bound in India by Thomson Press India Ltd.

CONTENTS

THE 53ᴿᴰ CARD

Every pack contains 52 playing cards, or so I was told by my parents. Playing cards were my first toys, like injections would be that of a doctor's child. My parents, ardent Bridge players of their times, champions in their own right, introduced me to a deck of cards at a very early age. They would conveniently remove an additional card, as all bridge players do, when they started playing. An additional card called the Joker.

It fascinated me from very early age. There was something about this card that held my attention. To my mind, a child's mind then, it was as if the card was winking at me. Waiting for me to discover its secrets. The Joker sometimes even surpasses an ace. If you ever played the game flash/teen Patti, you will know that a Joker can sometimes be a King, a Queen a Jack or an Ace, and sometimes it can even be a 2, in this case can defeat an Ace, if it is so strategically placed and A23 in your opponent's hand is definitely smaller than two 2s and one Joker in your hand. The trick therefore is not in the cards that you hold but how you play them. If you hold a Joker, where and how you use it, makes all the difference.

In Thoth Tarot deck, the Joker refers to a person, in a perfect state of joy and freedom, the sure feeling to be one with the spirit of life, at any time. Symbol of 0, for someone ready to go in any direction, open to all possibilities. He belongs nowhere, has no past, but has infinite future. The shape of an egg, the symbol of origin of life. A Joker is often a person who is undaunted by external influences. Our choices make the difference, but what is more important is the environment. The purpose of the joker's life therefore is to find his happiness in whatever he is doing, without letting external factors interfere, without letting situations deter him, and without letting anything come in the way of who he wants to be and what he wants to do.

Once you have found the purpose of your life, your Ikigai, you will know that everything else seems irrelevant. Finding that joy is a journey that you must embark on, for it leads to the fulfillment of your life. This book endeavors to help you find your Ikigai in a manner that is engaging while you are having fun. I write from personal experiences and I hope that you will have as much fun discovering your Ikigai as I did. I had the advantage of the right guidance at the right time. That is not to say I did not make mistakes, but here hoping you do not make the same mistakes that I did.

I hope this book will help you find your Ikigai.

ACKNOWLEDGEMENTS

Dedicated to Prabha and Prakash, mom and dad who taught me that a deck contains 52 cards.

To Nipun Arjun Bhatia who attended my workshop on Ikigai and inspired me to write a book on the same subject to reach out to the masses. For serving as a sounding board to bounce off ideas, as I conceptualized, wrote and re-wrote this book.

To my most precious friends Sonia Keswani and Lila Andrea Chaudhuri, for their love and support, and their impressive patience.

And finally to Mr. Dinesh Verma and his team of Pendown Press including Ritu, Faizan and Priya who kept pushing me to do my best!

CHAPTER 1

IKIGAI... A MYSTERIOUS WORD

Ikigai is a Japanese concept which roughly means "the happiness of always being busy." However, this phrase should not be read in a water-tight compartment as it goes beyond its literal meaning. It is also one of the secrets of the extraordinary longevity of the Japanese, especially on the island of Okinawa.

Those who delve deep and try to find the reasons why the inhabitants of this island outlive that of the people of anywhere else in the world, opine that it is Ikigai that shapes their life, along with a healthful diet, green tea and the conducive subtropical climate.

But again, the term Ikigai is not for Japanese only. In fact, all those who become successful to discover their Ikigai, get everything that they need, for a long and joyful journey throughout their life.

CHAPTER 2

IKIGAI REVEALED

If you get up each morning to take milk from the milkman, to open the door for the maid, to take your dog for a walk, congratulations ladies and gentlemen, you have found your Ikigai. The purpose of the book is solved.

Just kidding…

They say Ikigai is what wakes you up every morning. The above listed chores, that most of us hate getting up for, are most definitely not your Ikigai. My best friend Neetika, who would sit on the pot and give herself at least 10 reasons as to why she needed to go to college every single day. That was definitely not her Ikigai.

So, if Ikigai does not wake you up every morning what does it really do? Ikigai is your reason for being. They say, the greatest fear in the world is the fear of dying. In reality, what we are afraid that we will die and nobody will remember us, the fear of being insignificant. I was 3 years old, and living in a Bungalow in the tea plantation area of Dooars (foothills of Darjeeling), there were a lot of things I took for granted. Like massive manicured lawns, fruit orchard and vegetable garden in the house, pets and an abundance of servants. One day, as mom was working with the gardeners till particularly late in the evening, I saw the stars filling up the sky. I ran inside the house and stared crying. As Dad walked in, and saw me sobbing he asked me what had happened. As a child, I didn't know what exactly I was feeling, I didn't even know the word 'insignificant'. I just said, "the sky is so big and full of stars and I am so small."

Dad smiled, and in his wisdom took me out in the garden, pointed to a part of the sky, and asked, "What do you see there?" I looked, it was a dark patch of sky. "There are no stars there", I said. He smiled again, "that place is reserved for you, but you have to earn your way up there, nobody can take it from you."

The idea of finding your Ikigai is to find something that nobody can take away from you. something that helps you put bread on the table, something that makes you happy, something that brings you joy, something that you love doing and you're good at it, and something that helps you leave a living legacy so that you are remembered long after you are gone.

According to Japanese philosophers, only about 1/10th of people in the world have found their Ikigai.

Marc Winn used a Venn diagram to describe Ikigai. He recalled a diamond pattern of four circles with the word purpose in the center. He replaced the word purpose with Ikigai which is life's purpose. He does give us the most common representation of Ikigai, the four circled Venn diagram which pops up when you search Ikigai on Google.

But, Ikigai is not a Venn diagram. Tim Tamashiro calls Ikigai a map, a boomerang. He says do what you love, do what you're good at, and that's half your Ikigai. When you do what the world needs and what you can be rewarded for, it completes the full circle, the Ikigai circle of gifts. But Ikigai is neither a map, nor a boomerang. It's not even a circle. Ikigai is the point of intersection where your passion meets your profession.

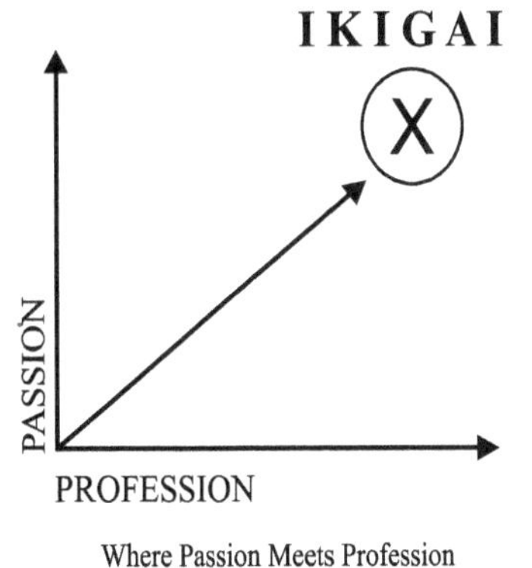

Where Passion Meets Profession

Step 2

To jump in and make it your profession to earn profit

Step 1

To observe without judging where your proficiency lies and what you're passionate about

Two Step Process

To observe without judging, from the eyes of the Joker and then to make it your profession. Those are the only two steps to Ikigai.

CHAPTER 3

IKIGAI TO YOU

When we talk about work-life balance, a lot of people will have the seemingly perfect jobs, seemingly perfect families, seemingly healthy lifestyles but still have this feeling of emptiness inside them. It is as if they're missing an important piece of their life, a seemingly important piece without which their life appears meaningless; their life appears to be a life without reason. Ikigai therefore is the reason for being; a life that drives you to be your best and leaves a living legacy.

I could see my father's image popping out of the scroll as the lawyer was reading my father's will, "Last will and testament of me, Prakash Arora," Where there is a will, I want to be in it. " To my darling daughter Reet, I leave, a boat." "A boat," said the devil sitting on my shoulder, "haven't you always dreamt of cruising the world in a small luxury boat, maybe it will even have a casino. There is the Sea Princess of your dreams and now you're going to get it" ...but the next words the lawyer said, ensured that my Sea Princess sank and the devil drowned in his tears. "Ah yes, Miss Arora", she said, "here's your boat." A paper boat!

That evening I went and watched the family videos that my father had made, hoping to find the secret of the paper boat.

The first video was taken when I was a few hours old. I imagine I had a hard life then, crying for food, crying for water, crying for a diaper change, braving those "ooh what a cute baby" from ogling aunts in different shapes and sizes, pinching my cheeks, "she has her mother's eyes, her mother's looks, and her father's... money." The love and pride that shone on my father's face as he held me for the first time and my little hand clasped his big finger... and the pain, when I bit it.

The next video was of a five year old Reet, who had rushed indoors at pitter-patter, the first drops of rain on the window-sill. My father said, "let me teach you how to make a paper boat", and with his deft fingers, he had carefully folded the paper to form a boat, hypnotic and beautiful . Father and daughter had stepped out in the rain, and set the boat adrift in the rushing muddy water, watching i toss from door to door. Dad created a legacy, one that would help me enjoy the monsoon, the rain water and paper boats forever.

Kabir has rightly said, - 'Kadli, seep, *bhujang mukh, swati ek gun teen*'. The first drop of rain, that falls into a Banana tree forms camphor, into an oyster forms a pearl, and into a serpent's mouth forms venom. Each one of us is as unique and precious as the first drop of rain. The legacy we leave behind, camphor, pearl or venom is our choice.

Margaret Thatcher got the legacy of 'commitment to service', from her father, a shopkeeper. A dyslexic child grew up to become General George Patton because his father left him 'courage to conquer'. 'Letters from a father to his daughter' made Pandit Nehru immortal not only for Indira Gandhi, but also for the world at large. Dr. Ralph C. Smedley's living legacy is a not-for-profit organization called Toastmasters International. These are the people who had found their Ikigai, and in the process left us timeless treasures.

Stretch out the palm of your hand and imagine your paper boat. Visualize it sailing smoothly over the waters. What is the paper boat that you are leaving behind?

CHAPTER 4

ANTI–AGING AND LONGEVITY

People who have found their Ikigai, are driven by the flow. They are the Jokers, leading meaningful lives. Therefore, it is not surprising that most of them live beyond 80, and many even beyond 100. This is the secret to the blue zones around the world including that of the Okinawa island in Japan. These people are too busy living their life purpose that they have no time to fall ill, or die.

Research shows that more than 50% of people in the world, hate their jobs, but do not have any plans of changing occupation. They are like the dog who sits on a nail and cries, that it's hurting, but doesn't get up from the nail because it's not hurting enough. Playing it safe means going along with the expectations of others, so that if they fail, they can blame others. If they are unhappy, it is the fault of the society.

Fear of failure makes us take jobs and adopt roles that we don't like. Gradually we start to behave according to the moulds that others have poured for us. We refuse to take risks, and we decline to stand out on our own two feet and go public with something a little out of the ordinary.

As children, we are uninhibited, we love chasing our dreams, chasing butterflies. We find simple tasks enjoyable, sometimes they even give us money. Arjun, at the age of 6 discovered his Ikigai. He was fond of reading Marvel comics and his parents bought him the entire collection. Now, Arjun had this huge friend circle who also liked reading Marvel comics, but couldn't afford to buy them whenever a new comic came into the market. Arjun realized an opportunity and devised a simple strategy that worked as a win-win situation for everyone. He started loaning out these comics to his friends at 50 paisa a week. At the age of 6, Arjun showed signs of not only being enterprising, when people are barely learning how to spell the word, but also was having fun in whatever he was doing. It was what the world needed, and he was getting paid for it.

As we grow up family pressure, peer pressure, pressure of societal norms, all inhibit us to live our lives according to what makes us happy. They push us in their framed notion of what is right or wrong according to generalized beliefs. So, the son of a businessman, must follow the family business, because it's set, easy, and tricks of trade can be passed along generations. Similarly, sons/grandsons of a lawyer must be good lawyers because the family has been doing law for generations. Sure enough, Arjun was caught by his mother in the process and she made him give up on making money from his friends. Was loaning comic books Arjun's Ikigai? At that age, probably yes. Could he continue doing that for the rest of his life? He may have continued lending books eventually opening a library, or even expanded to have his own publishing house. But we see that as we grow, in age, in experiences, in our thinking, our Ikigai changes, and that's okay.

I was representing my college, at an intercollegiate debate competition. I went to my teacher, Dr. Vibha Shetty and asked her if she would help me with a few pointers. She sat with me over a cup of tea and then told me "of course I can give you pointers, but then it will be my speech, do you still want it?" That hit my ego, I refused her help. The next day I went and smashed that debate competition. She was the first person to congratulate me, as I collected the winner's trophy. As she hugged me, she asked, "how do you feel?" I said "I feel great." I had managed to show her that I could win it even without her contribution. She smiled, " would you have felt the same if I had given you the points?"

Sometimes it is in that 'no' that we realize our best potential. She took me to Toastmasters International and that set me off on the journey from a doctor to becoming a TEDx speaker and a corporate trainer. I realized that my Ikigai was in helping people find their purpose in life. When times are hard and we suffer the pressure of being reasonable or denying our instincts, the Joker reminds us that our inner person knows best what to do.

My name is Pritish Acharya, and I have been a photographer for over a decade and a half. Sometimes I take up honorary assignments for a cause, and this was one such day. People would walk up to me with special request for pictures and group pictures, and I happily obliged.

At about 10.30am, as I was clicking yet another group picture, this lady dressed in a corporate attire, sprinted right into the camera frame, and the first thing that came out of her mouth was not an apology for disrupting the picture, but "That's not how you take a picture!" "Excuse me", said I, quite shocked by her audacity. Here I was, thinking I was the best photographer they could get, and this lady who just walked in, threw my claim out of the window. Would she now try to teach me how to click a photograph? Just who did she think she was? One thing was for sure, I would never click her picture.

Somewhere at the corner of my eye, I noticed her hugging all the people in the group and each of them smiling. Not the typical reaction one expects when you disrupt a group picture. Then, to my utmost surprise, she happily planted herself right in the middle of the group, held my camera lens, with a smile on her face, pointed to the group and said, "now this is how you take a picture, with me in it!" I went from shocked to pleasantly surprised when I realized she wasn't really questioning my skills as a photographer, but rather was just playing around and messing with her friends.

Today, several years later, I still tease Pritish with "that's not how you take a picture." As you have probably guessed, I was the girl shouting that out. Pritish found his Ikigai in shooting, and any interference to that flow is uncomfortable. Sometimes, you just have to be the Joker, and sometimes it's your friends who can be your eyes and observe without judging.

Lessons learnt:

1. Ikigai may change over a period of time, and that's okay.

2. Sometimes we find our ikigai and sometimes it is thrust on us.

3. It's in observing without judging that we truly find out where our Ikigai lies.

For those of you who are wondering what happened to Arjun, I believe he has found his Ikigai as a Business Counsellor.

CHAPTER 5

HOW TO FIND YOUR IKIGAI

Take time to answer these questions, write them down.

If you had the Joker's magic wand, how would you change the world? If you could go back in time and do one thing that could change your life, what would it be?

What do people usually call you for advice on (Observe as the Joker)

When was the last time you did something for the first time? How was it like to step out of your comfort zone and come out of the experience with the feeling of exhilaration/ excitement?

WHAT IF?

What if I'm not good enough? If we all waited till we were perfect in what we did, we wouldn't really be able to do anything much. What can help you become better, a book, a coach or a class?

"What if I quit my job?" If you're the bread winner of your family, don't quit your job until you're making more money from your hobby than from your job.

What if I fail? What have you got to lose?

"No, it can't be done," said people to a man named Thomas Alva Edison. Had he given up, today we would be still living in the dark.

"That's just impossible, man can't fly", said people to the two Wright brothers', and the Wright Brothers (Orville and Wilbur) proved people wrong. Ever boarded a flight?

At a state-level speech contest, with shaking feet and sweaty palms, I asked my mentor, "Do you think I should participate?" His answer was simple, "What have you got to lose?" Even with a second place, I had won! Overnight, I was the queen of the college with my picture in the papers, I had gained popularity, friends, experience and confidence.

A famous doha reads: *"Jin dhoondha tin pahiya, gehre paani paithi Main bhapura duban dara, raha kinare baithi,"* meaning "Those who strive, conquer by jumping into the waters, and I, scared of drowning, sit at the shore empty-handed."

Do we stop walking because we might fall, stop swimming, because we might drown, or stop driving, for the fear of having an accident? Then why do we stop believing in ourselves? Why do we stop taking more chances? Give yourself as many chances as you need to find your Ikigai.

Ever seen a toddler learn how to walk? Spreading both the arms across, with one wobbly step after another, a child falls down, gets up wobbles a little more, falls again, gets up… the process is repeated till the toddler finally starts walking and eventually running.

Has there been a time when you thought something would be impossible and now looking back it feels like childs' play?

August 2014 International Convention at Kuala Lampur Chris Woo, finalist at the World Champion of Public Speaking, came to the stage and spoke on how he didn't have a speech, and that it's okay to fail. It's okay to be imperfect, it's okay even if you don't do well today, because tomorrow…Tomorrow is another day. A very powerful and speculative ending from 'Gone With The Wind' by Margaret Mitchell. To me, it means another chance, to learn, to grow, to make mistakes, to learn from them and to grow some more. Another chance to find your Ikigai.

Grit, goal and an unrelenting zeal for work will help you find your Ikigai.

CHAPTER 6

A CINDERELLA STORY, RETOLD

DOES ONE SIZE REALLY FIT ALL?

My shoe size is 6, and today I belong to the rather long list of women with a 6 shoe size. I often wondered, 'What if Cinderella had a shoe size 6?' The result would've been the courtiers coming back to report, "Prince eighteen women and one man fit into the shoe, you can choose whom you want to marry, and the man is rather sweet looking".

If we were all similar, we would come in regular sizes, 5 X 4 or 6 X 5, which would mean 5 feet tall and 4 feet wide for a woman, 6 feet tall and 5 feet wide for a man. No more Mr. India or Miss World contests, no more getting that designer to specially design a dress for you (everything would be of your size), and no more spending endless hours on yoga/aerobics or exercise.

Men are often advised, 'Women are attracted by a little bit of mystery and unpredictability', and this more than often ends up in a man trying to be mysterious, unpredictable, but turning out to be outright weird. There goes the woman of your dreams, running out through the front door. Gentlemen, find what works for you, and your lady love. There is no 'one shoe fits all situation' in real life.

To me, a 'one shoe fits all' situation is like looking for a travel blog, and finding job placements, health, motivation, morbidity, share market, news, all stuffed on the same page. Just imagine the time you would waste in scanning through unnecessary stuff only because you decided to take a short trip.

"What is the secret of your success?" How many times have we looked at a successful person and wondered? What if I told you the magic that makes it work? While there may be guidelines to success, there is absolutely no sureshot method to prove than any method is foolproof. Also, if plan A works for a particular person, there is no reason to believe that plan B can't work for you. For all you know, you may need a plan Z.

Then there are the other extremes, 'Suresh is such a loser, he has a dream job, a dream wife and a dream car, yet he sulks all day'. Suresh may have a tax problem, or stress that kills him. Maybe your dreams are his nightmares, when he coughs up for maintenance. The key lies in knowing what you want and achieving to find it, and you do not need Cinderella's Fairy God Mother.

A former world contestant was advised before a championship, 'nobody wears jeans to a contest, you have to be in a business suit.' He wore the jeans, and he won. The magic lies in creating your own magical formula. Whether you are a size 6 or a size 4 or a size 11, whether you have flat feet, or arched ones, whether you prefer heels, or flats, you are unique. Find that unique shoe that fits you. Find your own Ikigai.

Joy Behar, known today as a former co-host on The View, was a High School English teacher who didn't launch her show business career until after age 40. Tim and Nina Zagat, the husband- wife team had each turned 42 before they gave up their legal careers to write their first restaurant guides. Their eponymous company is a part of Google now. Harland was a failure who got fired from a dozen jobs before starting his restaurant and then failed at that when he went out of business and found himself broke at the age of 65. Then Colonel Harland Sanders sold the first KFC franchise in 1962. It's never too late to start living a life full of purpose.

Find what's 'Uniquely You'. Find your Ikigai.

CHAPTER 7

BE YOUR OWN BRAND

My favorite stand up comedian talks about a time in his late 20s, when he had a relationship he didn't like, he had a job he didn't like and he had two roommates called 'Mom & Dad'. Then, he did something about it. 3 years later, he was without a girlfriend, he had job he didn't like and he had two roommates that made dumb and dumber look like Einstein and Newton. Today, several years and several professions later (including a failed Subway Sandwich shop), Darren LaCroix is one of the most successful stand up comedians of the world, a World Champion of Public Speaking, and one of the highest paid coaches in USA. Sometimes you find your Ikigai on the first try, and sometimes you need to keep trying again and again till you find it.

"Rajiv, your company is underrating our teas." Being the Executive Director of a Tea Company called Diana, my father had a problem. He felt that the tea that the company sold was underrated by the tea tasters. Rajiv looked at my Dad and said, "fine Prakash, I shall conduct a tea -tasting session myself tomorrow."

The next day, Rajiv walked into the house and waited patiently for my Dad to return from the garden to escort him to the factory. Meanwhile, the servants brought him a pot of tea, and he drained it to the very last cup. When my father arrived, he said, "I'm ready to go to the factory. Oh by the way, lovely tea, was it Darjeeling?"

For the uninitiated, Darjeeling produces some of the best teas in the world. My father smiled, he called the servant and said, "the tea that you served to Sir, get me 2 spoons of it." The servant quickly got it, my father pocketed it and off he went to the factory, with Rajiv in tow. There he asked Rajiv to pick up tea samples from the stacks randomly. He got them lined up, and then took out the sample from his pocket and got the brews prepared. Rajiv tasted each one, and gave each one a perfect score. My father had done it, a perfect 10 on 10. Soon enough Diana tea was the number one tea in the entire state.

To give you a bit of the background information, my Dad had left Duncans Goenka Group, to join a sick garden, Diana, because he believed that he could turn it around. From number 130 to the number 1 in tea, the road was long, full of toil. There were days and nights of hardwork, and more hard work. People told my father, "Prakash, you are kidding yourself, this garden will never amount to anything very much, it just can't be done!"

Have you ever been told by someone that something "just can't be done!?" What will you do about it?

This story was narrated to me by the same Rajiv at my father's deathbed. My father had found his Ikigai in manufacturing Tea.

"Ahsu, your new walkman, it's broken from the side, you bought it yesterday" cried my uncle, who had borrowed my cousin's walkman to listen to a song, as we drove down to Nepal. "No Dad, it was broken when we bought it", said Ashu. Back in the tea gardens, when my mother's expensive crockery went missing, she usually created havoc in the house, and hours later the servants came out with a chipped cup or saucer and a standard sheepish reply, "Memsaab, it was broken from before."

While most people all over the world fret over broken crockery, Nekchand found his Ikigai creating the Rock Garden, in Chandigarh, India, using the same pieces of broken crockery.

One man's misfortune may be another man's treasure, his Ikigai. Look around, do you see anything that interests you? Bring meaning to your life through your hidden Joker. Remember, the game ain't over till the last card is played!